TWEED JOURNEY

VALERIE GILLIES, JUDY STEEL AND SHELLEY KLEIN

Dedicated to Savourna Stevenson

CANONGATE

Acknowledgements

This book has arisen from The Tweed Journey project for the 1989 Borders Festival of Ballads and Legends, the central part of which was the new Suite for Clasarch and Ensemble by Savourna Stevenson. The exhibition from which the poems and photographs derive was made possible through the financial assistance of The Scottish Arts Council, the Borders Regional Council and the Borders Museums Forum comprising the District Council museums of Tweeddale, Ettrick and Lauderdale, and Roxburgh.

The authors would like to thank Michael Grieve for permission to reproduce two verses from Hugh MacDiarmid's *The Borders*; Felicity Ballantyne, Rosi Capper, Ian Brown and Rosemary Hannay. Thanks for help and inspiration are also due to Mr and Mrs Cockburn of Damhead Farm, Traquair, Mr W. Grey also of Traquair, Mr S. Dalgleish of Walkerburn, The Earl and Countess Haig of Bemersyde, Melrose, and finally to Walter Elliot of Selkirk.

First published in 1989
by Canongate Publishing Limited
17 Jeffrey Street, Edinburgh

Text © Judy Steel
Poems © Valerie Gillies
Photographs © Shelley Klein

Designed by Tim Robertson

British Library Cataloguing in Publication Data
Gillies, Valerie
Tweed journey
1. Great Britain. Tweed River region, history
I. Title.   II. Steel, Judy
941.3′7

ISBN 0-86241-263-3

Typeset by Speedspools, Edinburgh
Printed by Maclehose & Partners, Portsmouth

TWEED JOURNEY

CONTENTS

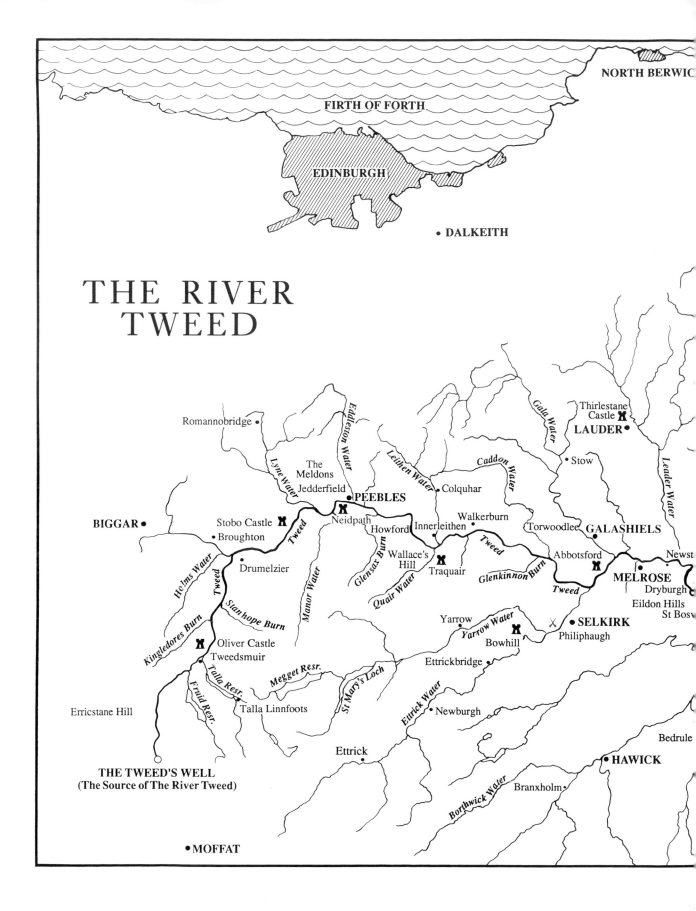

THE RIVER
TWEED

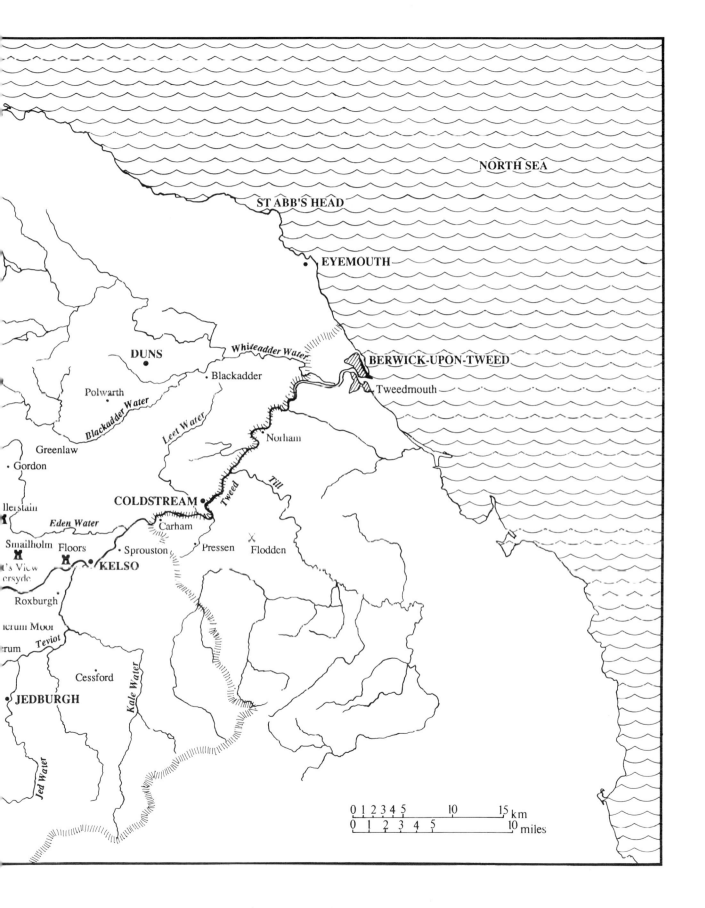

NORTH SEA

ST ABB'S HEAD

EYEMOUTH

Whiteadder Water

DUNS

• Blackadder

BERWICK-UPON-TWEED

Tweedmouth

Polwarth

Blackadder Water

Leet Water

Greenlaw

Norham

• Gordon

Tweed

Till

llerstain

COLDSTREAM

Eden Water

Carham

Smailholm   Floors

• Sprouston   • Pressen   ⚔ Flodden

's View

ersyde

KELSO

Roxburgh

erum Moor

Teviot

rum

Cessford

Kale Water

JEDBURGH

Jed Water

0 1 2 3 4 5   10   15 km
0 1 2 3 4 5   10 miles

A BRIEF HISTORY

Annan, Tweed and Clyde
Rise a' frae the ae hillside

So runs the jingle, and it is true that these three great rivers of the south of Scotland all have their sources remarkably close to one another some fifteen miles north of Tweedsmuir on the wild and majestic Edinburgh to Moffat road. But of these rivers it is only the Tweed that runs eastwards, on a journey that takes it on a near hundred-mile route before flowing into the North Sea at Berwick-on-Tweed. It runs not just through upland and moor, through forest and plain, but also through Scotland's history; and it is with the Romans that the known, or half-known story of man and woman in the Tweed valley begins.

Scattered evidence of Roman occupation has emerged over the centuries, but it was at Newstead, with the coming of the railway in 1843 and the excavations which followed that the promise of riches was uncovered. Here, almost midway along the Tweed's course, and beside the triple-peaked Eildon Hills that gave their settlement its name of Trimontium, they built and manned the fort that was crucial to the government of the Roman province of Valenta, peopled by the Votadini and Selgovae tribes. The attempt at colonisation beyond Hadrian's Wall was never successful for long: in five waves the Romans established themselves at Trimontium with over a thousand soldiers between the years 79 and 213 AD. But no period of occupation lasted for longer than twenty years.

The treasure trove they left is priceless, not in terms of gold and silver, but in what it tells us about the sketchy Roman occupation of Scotland. Here were brickworks and glassworks; here were altars and tombstones. One of them (translated) reads:

TO THE GOD SYLVANUS, FOR HIS OWN AND HIS SOLDIERS' SAFETY, CARRIUS DOMITIANUS, THE CENTURION OF THE TWENTIETH LEGION, SURNAMED THE VALIANT AND VICTORIOUS FULFILLS HIS VOW JUSTLY AND WILLINGLY.

The main excavation of Trimontium was carried out by a Melrose solicitor, Dr Curle, at the beginning of this century. Though an amateur archaeologist, he set new standards of excavation and deduction. Most of his discoveries are to be found in the National Museum of Antiquities in Edinburgh.

As elsewhere in Europe, with the withdrawal of the Romans, uncertainty shrouds the Borders. It is not even easy to date the unexplained remains that whet the appetite – the man-made caves cut into the Tweed's largest tributary, the Teviot, and four of the waters that feed it; the 'British camps' or forts of which there are seventy-six in Tweeddale district alone; the standing stones of Yarrow and the carved stones of the upper Ettrick; and the solitary broch at Torwoodlee between the Tweed and the Gala Water. These squat circular brochs proliferate in the North of Scotland; the Torwoodlee broch with its fragments of Roman pottery and late native Celtic articles is the only one in the south. But what of the people who lived there?

Tantalising, too, is the earthwork that runs from this broch, and spreads itself for nearly fifty miles throughout the region. It is a double-dyked ditch that would appear to have been thrown up for defensive reasons. Its construction is peculiar to itself and even its name, the Catrail, evokes a variety of explanations. From almost all of these archaeological conundrums there is much to learn, and much on which to speculate.

The Tweed and its tributaries have Arthurian claims: one of his battles is placed in the Ettrick Forest district, another in Wedale, on Gala Water. The Arthurian legend is claimed by many areas of Britain, but from what age comes the legend that it is beneath the Eildons that Arthur and his knights lie, not in death but in a kind of limbo, awaiting the summons to continue the struggle?

A stronger claim for the Tweed is its setting for the last wanderings of the semi-mythical figure of Merlin. A recent book by Nicholas Tolstoy, *The Quest for Merlin*, pinpoints, after detailed researches, the watershed of the Tweed as where the wizard lived, after fleeing from a final battle. And his burial place – after his death by stoning, staking and drowning – may be found at Drummelzier. An old prophecy foretold:

> When Tweed and Powsail meet at Merlin's grave, / Scotland and England that day one king shall have.

And it is said to have been fulfilled, for on the day of the coronation of James VI of Scots as James I of England, an unusually large flood joined the Tweed with its tributary at that precise spot.

From such myth and legend let us turn with more certainty to the written testimony of Bede for the next phase in the history of the Tweed – the coming of Christianity. In the seventh century the river lay in the kingdom of Northumbria and it was in the seven years of Oswald's reign (635–642 AD) that this ancient kingdom was converted to Christianity. Oswald's Christianity was the Celtic rather than the Roman influence: he himself had spent some formative years on the holy isle of Iona. He recruited the evangelising monk, Aidan, to carry out the work of spreading the Word throughout his kingdom, but it was Boisil, not Aidan, who was sent northwards from Northumberland's holy isle of Lindisfarne to the Tweed. He came to Mailros, not the Melrose of later centuries, but a settlement on that promontory of land within the horseshoe swept out by the river at the spot known today as Scott's View. There Boisil established the first religious community in the area.

But it was Boisil's protégé, Cuthbert, who did the greatest missionary work on the Tweed. As a shepherd on the upper reaches of the Leader Water, he had a vision which inspired him to seek out Boisil's monastery at Mailros. It is said that the Abbot recognised the boy's sanctity on sight and greeted him as one who would achieve great things. This Cuthbert certainly did, preaching the word of God to the people along the Tweed in their own tongue, achieving what were regarded as miracles, and drawing the love of all who came into contact with him. In due course he presided over Lindisfarne, and became the region's one native saint.

Cuthbert's story as recorded by Bede, is a welcome shaft of light in the murk of early Border history. The tales of the Culdean saint, Ronan, at the town of Innerleithen are more apocryphal – he is alleged to have cleiked (caught) the devil with a crook.

For a couple of centuries little is known of the area; even the history of Northumbria itself becomes shadowy. Then in 1018 came the first of many decisive battles to be fought along the banks of the Tweed, at Carham, east of Kelso on the south bank of the river. Here, Malcolm II of Scots triumphed, and the land known as Lothian and stretching to the Tweed was brought permanently within the boundary of Scotland. The river's strategic importance would never again be less than paramount.

Though any border area was bound to suffer some disturbance in those times, the eleventh and twelfth centuries appear to have been comparatively peaceful compared to those that followed. It was during this period that we first hear of the Border towns that we know today though of the greatest of them, Roxburgh, there is almost no trace. Roxburgh stood on the confluence of the Tweed and Teviot. It was a royal residence, a mighty fortress and a substantial town that included schools, three churches, and the Royal Mint. All but a few crumbling walls have disappeared as surely as a land-locked Atlantis. Roxburgh's demise, however, was man- or rather woman-ordained, and belongs to a later century. The reasons for it will emerge with the more turbulent history of those times.

The twelfth century establishment of the abbeys along the Tweed is another pointer to the tranquillity of that time. It was David I who granted the charters that sent the Tironensian monks first to Schelechirche (Selkirk) and after a few years transferred them to Calchou (Kelso); he also established the Cistercians at Melrose, the Augustinians at Jeddewrtha (Jedburgh), and the Premonstratensians at Dryburgh. He gave the monks, too, wealthy tracts of land to support their abbeys – land that the Scots Crown could ill afford. 'A sair sanct for the crown' his successors called him, bemoaning the impoverishment of their inheritance.

The monks became the Tweed's first systematic farmers, especially at Kelso and Melrose. It was at the Abbey of Melrose that the Cistercians began a mammoth and priceless record of the history of their own and earlier times. *The Chronica de Mailros* begins in 735 AD with a retrospective record that becomes a contemporary account between 1140 to its sudden end in 1270.

The Abbeys stand ruined now and what may be seen of them are in fact reconstructions, carried out when the original edifices suffered destruction and disintegration. But their one-time grandeur can still be conjured up in the mind's eye as can their importance in the sparsely populated country that was Scotland. Built so near to the border, they express an optimism in the country's relations with its larger southern neighbour, and the Border towns, some with favoured royal residences, expanded around them.

There was another reason for David I's confidence in placing the abbeys here. He did not in all probability see the Tweed as the future boundary of his kingdom. Through his wife, Mathilda, daughter of the Earl of Northumberland, he held the three counties south of the Border, as far as Skipton in Yorkshire. The likelihood of their permanent absorption into the Scottish Crown was a strong one and would have had the added advantage of making the two nations more equal in size, with the Tyne or the Tees forming the march (or border) rather than the Tweed.

But Henry II of England demanded the return of those counties and their powerful castles from David's successor, who was not strong enough to resist. The possession of them became a source of dispute to succeeding generations, and the lands around the Tweed and its tributaries began to suffer from the effects of being a battleground; a situation that was to persist, with periods of remission and differing degrees of intensity, for nearly five centuries.

The thirteenth century by and large – and certainly in relation to those that followed – was for Scotland a golden age. It was the time of those two real-life characters who have given so much to the folklore and balladry of the Tweed: Thomas the Rhymer, or Thomas Learmouth of Ercildoune, poet, mystic and prophet. The other was Michael Scott, traveller, scholar, alchemist and, so it was believed, practitioner in the black arts.

It was the time too of the rise of Berwick-on-Tweed during the reigns of Alexander II and III, a period that lasted for seven decades. At the time Berwick promised to develop into the major port not just of Scotland but of the entire island of Britain. Perhaps paying a compliment to the names of the Scots kings, a contemporary chronicler described Berwick's bustle and wealth as giving it the air of a northern Alexandria 'for its walls, its waters, its wealth the sea'. At the end of that period, the customs duties which the town surrendered to the Scots exchequer in wool and hide alone came to more than one quarter of the entire export duties paid by all English ports to their exchequer. The habitual poverty attributed to pre-union Scotland does not seem to have afflicted her at this time. She stood on a relatively equal and peaceful footing with England, and Berwick merchants looked confidently east to the Low Countries and Scandinavia.

As the end of the century approached, there appeared to be only one cloud on the horizon: the lack of a suitable successor to Alexander III. His only heir was his young grand-daughter Margaret, daughter of the King of Norway. But Alexander, though not in the first flush of youth, was healthy and virile. In 1285 as the guests made their way along the Tweed and by the Teviot and Jedwater to his marriage with the young French Yolande at Jedburgh, the lack of male heirs, born and raised on native soil, must have seemed a short-term problem.

It is said that the marriage festivities were brought to an abrupt end with the intrusion of a skeletal dancer among the revellers. It is a fact that within a few months Alexander III died in an accident without having impregnated Yolande. The twelve-year-old Maid of Norway, now Queen Margaret, was sent for, but died in the Orkneys of a childish ailment on the way to claim her inheritance – not, as told in the ballad of Sir Patrick Spens, in a storm a 'half-hour from Aberdour'.

There were twenty claimants for the succession. Scotland was plunged into a constitutional crisis, a struggle from which she barely emerged with her nationhood intact. In the drama played out over the next decades, the Tweed was the setting for many scenes of high tension, of inspiration, of tragedy, and, from time to time, of farce.

The Maid of Norway had been promised in marriage to the son of Edward I of England and it was he whom the guardians of Scotland now approached to settle the claims of the competitors. In the early summer of 1291, a council was convened at Norham by the banks of the Tweed and as a preliminary, Edward demanded recognition of his status as 'Lord-paramount' of Scotland. The weakness with which the Scots commissioners agreed to this can be explained by a variety of motives, but it is still not pardonable.

Seventeen months later, in the great hall at Berwick (the spot is now the railway station of Berwick-on-Tweed), Edward delivered his judgement in favour of the puppet king, John Balliol. Three days later, again at Norham, Balliol paid homage to Edward for the nation of Scotland.

Within a few years Edward showed what he meant by being 'Lord-paramount'. An attempt by the Scots to show some muscle by allying themselves with France against England brought him north with a substantial, efficient and brutal army. The first hammer blows were raised on Berwick which was sacked with a savagery that would appal us even today. Estimates of the slaughtered were as high as 15,000 – half of Berwick's twentieth-century population. Included in the casualties was a woman in the very act of childbirth.

For the next four months Edward waged war

throughout Scotland, demanding and receiving from all who mattered recognition of his claim as overlord. When he returned to Berwick in August, almost every Border family appears on the list in the Ragman Roll as having sworn allegiance to him. Heading it were the Abbots of 'Jeddeworthe, Meuros and Kelschou'.

But if the capitulation of the Scots was nowhere more complete than along the lower reaches of the Tweed, in the area surrounding one of its tributaries the movement for resistance was nurtured. To Ettrick Forest came the defiant William Wallace with a small band of followers, augmented by the archers of that area. Later it was at St Mary's Kirk that he was proclaimed Guardian of Scotland. His mission was joined, after some prevarication, by Sir Simon Fraser of the upper Tweed valley, who rode out from Neidpath Castle to join him, first in victory, then in defeat, and finally in the shameful death that Edward devised for those he considered rebels. To the Tweedside castles of Berwick and Roxburgh the English king sent the dismembered limbs of Wallace, to act as a deterrent to others who might oppose him.

By 1306 Scotland was truly an occupied country. The south was especially well policed. Edward, whose tomb bears the simple inscription MALLEUS SCOTORUM (hammer of the Scots) could have been forgiven for believing that, with Wallace's death, his conquest of Scotland was complete. But, phoenix-like, there emerged Robert Bruce, Earl of Carrick, who could claim not just leadership but kingship of his fellow Scots. On the way to his hurried coronation at Scone, Bruce had a meeting at Tweed's Cross at the summit of the pass at Erricstaine near the source of the Tweed, an encounter that was to prove both decisive and fruitful. It was with the young man who was to become his most trusted colleague and lieutenant, Sir James Douglas.

Amongst those who pursued Scotland's cause to its triumphant conclusion nearly three decades later, Douglas was the one leader who was completely uncontaminated by a former fealty to Edward. He was a romantic figure whose imaginative and mainly successful exploits often brought him to the Tweed. Of all his adventures, perhaps the capture of Roxburgh Castle was the most audacious and makes the best story.

The possession of it was the key to the control of the border and the English had managed to retain this until 1314. Douglas mixed psychology with daring in his plans. Choosing Shrove Tuesday for the assault, on the assumption that the garrison would be 'merrymaking', Douglas and his men disguised themselves in black coverings and crept on hands and knees towards the castle in the dusk. In this manner, Douglas hoped, any non-merrymaking sentinel would mistake them for cattle. The ruse worked, the assault was successful, and the capture of Roxburgh strengthened Bruce's hand immeasurably in the run up to the decisive Battle of Bannockburn.

It is often assumed that this battle marked the end of the hostilities and that all Scotland had by then fallen to Bruce. But Berwick remained in English hands for longer and the final treaty was not signed for another fifteen years. It was here, too, that the Countess of Mar was imprisoned in a cage by Edward in the most appalling conditions as retribution for her part in Bruce's defiant coronation.

The events that plunged Scotland into the bitter struggle for existence began at Norham and at Berwick, and it was there too that the circle closed. To Norham, where the Scots lords had acknowledged Edward's claim as 'Lord-paramount' of Scotland, came an embassy from that king's grandson, Edward III, acknowledging Scotland again as a free and equal nation. At Berwick, where John Balliol had been adjudged king, the marriage took place between Bruce's young son David, and Joan, daughter of Edward III. Until he sent his embassy to Norham, Edward had referred to the Scots king as 'the rebel Robert de Brus, lately Earl of Carrick'. Now he became 'the magnificent Prince Sir Robert, by the grace of God King of Scots, his dearest friend'.

The Tweed's connection with Bruce and Douglas cannot be concluded without the post-script that tells how it was that the king's heart is buried at his favoured abbey of Melrose. Bruce had vowed to go on a crusade but by the time the events referred to had taken place he was already dying of leprosy. He begged Douglas to fulfil the vow by taking his embalmed heart to the Holy Land and the arrangements were duly made after his death. But Douglas, veteran of so many battles and skirmishes in Scotland, fell on Spanish soil. It is said that, when surrounded by Saracens, he threw the casket into the heart of the conflict with the words, 'Lead on brave heart, as thou wert wont to do, and I shall follow'. The body of the one hero and the heart of the other were recovered and returned to their chosen resting places.

The Treaty of Northampton ratified by Bruce and Edward should have secured peace between the nations and respite for the beleaguered inhabitants of the frontier land. But throughout the fourteenth and fifteenth centuries under the weak Scots government, invasion and counter-invasion, raid and counter-raid continued. Territorial gains were made and lost, castles taken and retaken, truces made and broken. It was all unedifying and pointless. In time, this ceaseless tramp of armies had its effect on the people who lived there. As their homes and goods and indeed families were treated with such indifference by those acting under official command, so they began to lose respect for law and order, evolving their own codes of conduct and reaping the benefits of the un-settled state of the countryside in which they lived.

On his return to his faction-torn kingdom after nearly twenty years' imprisonment in England, James I sought to remedy matters. His admirable and simple policy, 'to make the key keep the castle and the bracken bush the cow' was nowhere more needed than in the Borders. The treaty he signed at Melrose in 1424 included a code of Border laws and contained much good sense in attempting to work out a *modus vivendi* that would bring stability and justice to a notoriously difficult situation. It depended on international good-will, and during James' reign at least, this existed.

From this period we have an unflattering portrait of the Tweed valley from a young Italian traveller, later Pope Pius II. His negative impressions mirror those of the French soldiers who in the previous century had been sent to assist the Scots army on the border and had returned home as soon as they could decently do so. The future pope admired the women of the region, both for their looks and their friendliness, but found the men small and short-tempered. He chronicled the poverty of the towns and villages and the starkness of the landscape, describing it as 'rugged, uncultured, and in winter inaccessible to the sun's rays, has no feature in common with my home'. One of his other comments still rings true today – that nothing pleases the Scots so much as to hear abuse of the English.

From James himself we have a different picture altogether of the inhabitants of Tweedside. The poet-king observed the celebrations of his subjects in Peebles of their fair day:

At Beltane, when ilk bodie bownis
To Peblis at the play,
To heir the singing and the soundis

The solace, such to say,
Be furth and forest furth they found
They graythit them full gay,
God wat that wold they do that stound
For it was their feist day
They said
Of Peblis to the play.

While the burgesses got on with everyday life,
power struggles raged around them. Now it was
less between Scotland and England than between
the Scots crown and the all-powerful house of
Douglas. The latter had acquired, through royal
favour, advantageous marriages and opportunism,
lands and possessions throughout the country that
made it a real rival to the royal house itself. The
eighth earl's confirmatory grant from James II contained, in the area of the Tweed and its tributaries
alone, the wardenship of the West and Middle
Marches, the forests of Selkirk and Ettrick, Sprouston, Hawick, Bedrule, Smailholm, Romanno,
Kingsmeadow, Glenwhilm and Lauderdale, and
the castles of Newark and Hermitage.

James II eventually brought down the house of
Douglas. The eighth earl was assassinated and the
king (in whose reign a second, more refined code
of Border laws was promulgated) could now turn
his attention to the recapture of the castles of
Berwick and Roxburgh, still in English hands.

The absorption of that nation in the self-
destructive Wars of the Roses gave James his
opportunity; in 1460 he laid seige to Roxburgh.
The king was something of a student of munitions
and was deeply interested in the new forms of
explosive cannon. He was supervising the dis-
charge of one of these at the siege when it acci-
dentally exploded, killing him immediately. He was
only thirty and had had some of the better characteristics of the Stewart monarchs, including their
ability to communicate with, and inspire, the

people. This was a gift shared by his widow, Mary
of Gueldres, who arrived on the scene with their
eight-year-old son and arranged his coronation in
Kelso Abbey as James III. She personally super
vised the successful conclusion of the seige, and
then ordered the complete dismantling of the
mighty Castle of Roxburgh. Built to defend Scotland, it had all too often become a wooden horse
for the English, and Mary's decision was the cor-
rect one in strategic terms. But what a radical
change for the people of the Tweed and Teviot the
removal of that edifice must have been, having for
so many centuries shaped the lives of those in its
shadow.

The twenty-eight year reign was an unhappy one
for the new boy king but a peaceable one for the
nation. Cross-border warfare remained at a low
ebb and an uneasy peace reigned. The main events
in the power struggle between James III and
his nobles took place well to the North, but one
horrific, brief scene was enacted on the Leader
Water, one of the Tweed's tributaries. There, over
Lauder Brig, the rebellious lords hanged the king's
favourites despite his pleading and tears. They
were men of low birth but of the artistic tempera-
ment that James preferred for company. In the
more cultured climate of mainland Europe he
might have been hailed as a Renaissance prince, in
fifteenth-century Scotland he was overthrown and
murdered.

Under his son, James IV, Scotland approached
the sixteenth century, the most tumultuous of her
existence. As the young princess Margaret Tudor
crossed the Tweed en route to her marriage to the
charismatic and able Scots king in 1502, the omens
of peace, which meant prosperity for the Tweed,
looked promising. James would be son-in-law to
Henry VII of England, brother-in-law to his sons
of whom only the younger was to survive – the

formidable Henry VIII. Thoughts of the Stewart succession to the English throne as a result of this marriage must have been considerably less prominent than those of a peaceful alliance not only between England and Scotland but France and Spain, Scotland playing a central role in the newborn concept 'the balance of power'.

Sadly, almost a decade later, this delicate alliance was once again under threat. In 1513 Henry VIII attacked France, Scotland's traditional ally. James' rash but chivalric response to the French Queen's appeal for help was to have disastrous consequences for his country. In the summer of that year, with the most magnificent army ever mustered in Scotland, James IV crossed the Tweed and invaded his brother-in-law's territory.

The result, on a hillside by the Tweed's Northumbrian tributary the Till, was the most appalling catastrophe of all time for Scotland: the Battle of Flodden. The irony of it was that in terms of national defence it was utterly unnecessary. The affliction to Scotland was the more total because of the king's popularity; as the Hawick poet R. S. Craig put it: *They failed not at the summons, who knew the black mistake.* The flower of Scotland's manhood – the Archbishop of St Andrews, thirteen earls, fifteen lords and heads of clans, and many of their heirs, educated to the standard demanded in statute by James, fell with their king. So too did over 10,000 men of lesser rank, but of no less importance to their families, their villages, their burghs.

Flodden is a battle that never loses its pathos, not just on the Tweed and in Ettrick Forest, whence 'the Floo'ers o' the Forest were a' wede awa', but on occasions of mourning in all corners of the world where the haunting lament that commemorates it is still played. Its roots though are in the small town of Selkirk. Eighty of its men went to fight, one returned. This overwhelming loss is remembered each year at the Common Riding in a dramatic spectacle of horse and rider and banner.

In the years after Flodden, the Scots were worse enemies to themselves than were the English. As factions of nobles vied for power through the custody of the latest boy king, James V, so lawlessness mushroomed. The standards of the great abbeys declined; the transfer of their control and their wealth, to lay commendators rather than to religious heads, hastened their decay. This in turn was one of the causes of the Reformation which, it should never be forgotten, was for Scotland in the nature of a revolution, leading as it did to the overthrow of the established government.

A blood feud, begun by the banks of the Tweed near Melrose between the two most powerful families on the Border, the Scotts of Buccleuch and the Kerrs of Cessford, lasted for over forty years, and only served to increase the conditions for lawlessness. Throughout all this, the Border reivers, romanticised by later ballad makers and storytellers, rode out on expeditions as and when the need or inclination took them, returning resplendent with their booty. The Tweed valley itself was less populated with reiving families than the land surrounding its tributaries. An idea of how the wild men of Liddesdale were regarded may be gleaned from Sir Richard Maitland of Lethington's long 'Complaint against the Theives of Liddesdale', which begins:

> Of Liddesdale the common Theives
> So partly steals now and reives
> That none who keep
> Horse, nolt (cattle) or sheep
> Not yet dare sleep
> For their mischiefs.

After James V's early death his daughter, the week-old Mary, became Queen of Scots. Henry

VIII plotted the same course for her as Edward I had proposed two and a half centuries earlier the Maid of Norway: marriage to the Prince of Wales which would in effect bring England the dowry of Scotland. The Scots lords agreed, but within a year they had reneged.

There began an invasion of Scotland equal only to Edward's, known as the 'rough wooing'. Though Henry's armies stretched as far north as Tayside, it was the south that bore the brunt. On the Tweed's lower reaches, the fertile Merse known as 'the granary of Scotland' was devastated. The beautiful abbeys were all destroyed never to rise again and their surrounding towns were savaged. Tweeddale and Teviotdale suffered horrendously. In the words of Walter Scott of Branxholm, who suffered perhaps the heaviest losses, 'Teviotdale was burnt to the bottom of Hell'. He and Kerr of Cessford briefly put aside their blood feud and joined forces in one of the few successful Scottish engagements of the war, at Ancrum Moor in 1545, which helped to stem the tide until the arrival of French troops and the departure of the young Mary Queen of Scots to the safety of France.

When that ill-starred, romantic figure returned as a widow to Scotland she made royal progresses as far north as Inverness and as far west as Galloway. She visited Tweedside rarely: to Traquair on a hunting expedition, to Neidpath, and through Melrose on her way to administer justice at Jedburgh. She nearly died there after an arduous and wet journey on horseback to visit her wounded Lieutenant of the Border, Bothwell. In her later years of imprisonment she would repeat the phrase, 'Would that I had died at Jeddart'. What an unstained and uncontroversial figure she would then have been! During what can only have been a convalescence, she continued her Border progress to Kelso and thence to Berwick, where the Mayor greeted her from the town walls.

Mary's father, James V, had been a more frequent visitor both for law enforcement and for recreation. It was in his reign that the building of peel towers became mandatory. Many of them had been erected in previous centuries; now all holders of land of any substance were obliged to do so. These towers were useful for both defence and signalling; they now ranged the length of the Tweed from Oliver Castle near its source to Berwick. James V, and at a later date Mary's son, James VI, granted or confirmed the charters of such towns as Selkirk and Peebles. Today the colourful celebrations of Selkirk Common Riding and the Peebles Beltane Festival continue to carry out conditions such as the inspection of the boundaries of the towns' common land on horseback (the riding of the marches) as laid down in those charters.

The lawlessness and reiving of the area continued throughout the century – the last cross-border skirmish was in 1575 – but the days of both were numbered. No other region was so radically altered by the effects of the union of the two kingdoms under James VI as its status as a perpetual battleground drew to a close.

There seems some significance in the lack of involvement of the people of the Tweed both in the religious wars of the seventeenth century and the Jacobite risings of the eighteenth. The townspeople were able to go about their business without fear and the great families moved out of their simple, defensive tower houses and scattered the banks of the Tweed and its tributaries with the great historic homes that can still be seen today. Perhaps the most splendid of these is Floors Castle at Kelso, where the Kerrs of Cessford employed Sir John Vanburgh to build them a home in a style

appropriate to their newly acquired dukedom of Roxburghe.

There were incidents and events that belong to the Civil Wars however. A major conference of Covenanters was held at Talla Linns, near Tweedsmuir (which also boasts the area's only marked covenanter's grave) while on a tributary at the far end of the river, the Whiteadder, the young Grizel Hume concealed her fugitive father in the crypt of Polwarth Kirk and carried secret messages for him to his imprisoned confederate. As allies of the Covenanters, Cromwell's troops occupied Peebles, and Neidpath Castle surrendered for the only time in its history – without a shot being exchanged.

During the Civil Wars of both the seventeenth and eighteenth centuries it is Traquair House, near Innerleithen, that carries perhaps the strongest legacy. To it, the romantic Marquis of Montrose fled after his final defeat at Philiphaugh, by Selkirk; through its gates, opened for the last time, rode Prince Charles Edward Stuart a century later in an equally doomed cause. But the men that followed them were not, for the most part, from the Borders. They were more peaceably employed on humbler matters and the late eighteenth century was to see some of the fruits of their endeavours.

The knitting frame in Hawick was introduced in 1771. Twenty years later the first woollen mill was set up in Galashiels. Though hosiery and weaving had existed in this sheep intensive area before, this period marked the beginning of the industrial development of the towns along the Tweed, and throughout the nineteenth century. Hand in hand with it went the movement for electoral reform in which the Border towns played a lively, vociferous, and occasionally violent part.

Another significant event of the late eighteenth century was to place the land and its people irrevocably on the literary map. It was the arrival of a sickly Edinburgh boy to his grandfather's farm between St Boswells and Kelso. Beneath Smailholm Tower the imagination of the young Walter Scott was first stirred, and no name is more associated with the River Tweed than his. After his boyhood at Smailholm and later at Kelso, he lived first at Ashiesteil near Clovenfords, and then at the house he built with such love and cost to himself, Abbotsford. It was there that he died in 1832. His son-in-law and biographer, Lockhart, reflected that Scott's last sensation must have been the sound of the Tweed as it flowed past the open window.

Through Scott, the ballads and oral history of the region were given to a wider world. Through his romantic poetry and novels he can be said to have influenced a whole European movement. Few writers have stamped their identity so firmly on their own country or have contributed so much, for better or for worse, to how it is perceived by others.

A galaxy of writers followed Scott. Leading English poets and artists came to celebrate with him the countryside he wanted others to share. Turner was one of these, and his drawings and paintings of the old abbeys, castles, and towers such as Dryburgh and Earl Haig's Bemersyde have left subsequent generations with a strong image of the beauty and tranquillity of the Tweed in its Border setting.

But for those who love this Border country, the truly indigenous writer and the one they claim for their own is James Hogg. Born in the Ettrick valley in 1770, his stories and poems leave an unsurpassed legacy. Moreover, his great novel, *Confessions of a Justified Sinner*, portrayed to the world the conflicting characteristics of the Scots themselves.

John Buchan's name too is irrevocably associated with the Border country. He ranks as one of Scott's best biographers and, like Scott, was not actually born on the Tweed but spent his formative boyhood years there on his grandfather's farm near Tweedsmuir. Many of his thrillers, and particularly his historical novels and short stories are set in this wild inland Border country.

The nineteenth century saw the rise of the high quality tweed and hosiery industries in towns situated on the Tweed. The present century has alas seen the rationalisation of this, but the great names of Pringle, Ballantyne, Lyle and Scott, and Braemar are still known the world over; the garments that bear these names come from the towns on the Tweed and the Teviot. The Galashiels woollen trade barely exists now, though the town still provides the best training in the textile industry that Britain can boast.

The Border country was also opened up to a wider world in the eighteenth century by improved communications. The railway sliced out the 'Waverley Route' and Napoleonic prisoners of war were kept busy on various civil engineering feats. Many of the fine bridges over the Tweed, such as James Rennie's at Kelso, date from this period. The present century has seen the further opening up of the Borders by road, but the loss of the railway was a damaging blow.

The late twentieth century has seen the diversification of industry, the expansion of tourism in this, one of the last unspoilt parts of Britain, and radical changes in the pattern of farming and land use. Mechanisation and the reduction of employment on the farms has been one of these, though it is difficult to visualise how any invention can replace the renowned skill of the Border shepherd. Another introduction has been the growth of forestry – not the planting of the native species of birch, oak and Scots pine that once formed the great forests of the region, but the serried ranks of quick-growing conifers that obscure the beautiful undulating hills.

But the past still has its present day echoes:

O dinna fear the auld spirit's deid,
Gang to Selkirk or Hawick or Langholm yet
At Common-Riding time – like a tidal wave
it boils up again, and carries a' afore it.

Or in the seven-a-side Rugby games
Translated into terms o' skilfu' rivalry
The keen combative spirit of the Borderers still
Races and chases as aince on Canonbie Lea.

So wrote Hugh MacDiarmid in 1966 in his poem *The Borders*. He was right. You will find it in these settings. I have found it too at election times. And you will find it in the fusion of the past with the present, the ever-constant knowledge of roots in the poetry of today's Tweed Journey.

THE
POEMS

UPLAND SONG

Wind and wave, wind and wave,
river and banks, river and banks,
flood and growths, floods and growths,
moor and girl, stream and boy,
coulter and furrow, coulter and furrow,
shepherd and flock, dyker and stones,
grey-blue cattle, grey-blue cattle,
hawk and shaw, hound and course,
ring and fort, brig and fords,
it's a light loam, it's all white ground,
river and banks, river and banks,
wind and wave, wind and wave.

STREAM RHYTHM

The Powskein, the knife-slash,
then Cor Water, the long marsh,
Badlieu, all mossy-grey,
a wet spot through the day,
Smid Hope, the blacksmith's yards,
Glencraigie, rock-hard,
Fingland, with white gravel,
shining on bright pebbles,
and Hawkshaw, if it could talk,
the haunt of the hunting hawk.
Fruid water, the running one,
swift flow in shallow current,
Glenbreck, in speckled folds,
Glenwhappen, the whaup calls.
Menzion, at the standing stones,
Talla, the waterfall foams,
Gameshope, a winter month,
back of the wind, a shivery one,
Glencotho where the cuckoo's heard,
Glenrusco whose skin is fair,
bark from wood, the stripping-bare,
Kirk Burn of the grouse hen,
the hare's stone at Hearthstane,

Glenheurie has the yew wood.
The wolfhunt land is at Polmood
where Kings came to hold assize,
every kind of fruit tree thrives.
Kingledores, the champion's gateway,
Holms' meadows, islands of greenery.
Hopecarton, old fort in the midden,
Drumelzier, Medlar's dun is hidden.
The Scrape Burn, the gash in the hill,
a rough scart, see it you will,
the little Louran, a chatterbox burn,
the loud voice, the shouting one.
Manor's stony settlements rise,
Posso the pleasance, earthly paradise,
Hundleshope and Waddenshope,
a man's name in hollow court.

Time passing, blooms in places,
people there tell differences
on the ground by a tributary,
name a feature, give stability.
It's for a man who's not yet born,
it's a place for a future dawn.

THE BELTANE FORDING

Riders packed like a glacier
sweep onto the valley-floor,
a herd, a horde, a new element poured

where the grey horse running out
is Peebles' own White Stane, erratic.
Hard as ice, impervious hooves.

Horses in the water, fording
by the paved causeway, are plunging
to the sound a stone makes when struck.

Bridle the Tweed with a steel bit.
Sweaty foam from a dun horse
gaping, creams on the wave.

A boy is restraining his horse:
the river's split spiky case
reveals the fruit, horse-chestnut.

Now a huge cuff of current,
a wide anklet, swings over springy legs,
Pegasus has fetlocks winged with water.

And someone always falls off,
a falling weight reaching its natural state
whether swept away or not.

Stragglers cling on by their skins
to strap or saddle, mane or reins,
to the watershed of bellybands.

They're through even faster.
Bruised water of crumpled pewter
flows in on their hoofprints.

For the hoof hews a form
like a jaw, a round gum.
Upstream is a vanished tribal town,

Carbantorigon, the slope of the chariots,
whose hard wicker shapes survive
as these ghosts in the soil.

The people, the horses, the river
all make tracks together,
a wild band of followers.

OLD HOWFORD

One a.m. now
and what a row!
The owl is hooting encores
above the roof at Old Howford.

'Don't let the air
in anywhere!'
Lips to tight-cupped hands, I show
the boys how to follow his continuo.

Nearer the place,
his man-like face,
while they try to fix the sound as it is:
Echo is here, the lad of the cliffs.

MRS COCKBURN'S FAVOURITE

Once the forest of wolf and bear,
Scrub and loppings were burnt and cleared
To put the land in good heart
On green Damhead Rig.
Now this is a place that can impart
The world's good in a wonderful sweet air.
Your horse lifts his hooves with vigour,
Neatly for pleasure here.
Other places go to the bad,
Dark Glengaber, and deep Hannel Bog.
Only here the sun shines on green turf
And you raise healthy stock,
Trevana Knowe swings round its even curve;
Lucky the woman who is landlocked.

WALTER ELLIOT'S REEL

As everyone who ever danced
    Hears both pipe and horn
Birl the pirn, his tractor overturns
    But Walter rolls up reborn.

He stays a good while in the field.
    He often walks to search
For flints of chert, a chip, a glint
    Among the frosty earth.

And now he hears two rivers sing
    Their fervent radiant song.
Right by the water's edge he knows
    Sound carries them along.

Time past with present quarrelling
    Keeps separate in a huff:
Who was timberman and fencer
    Knows them well enough.

A Mesopotamia lies between
    The Ettrick and the Tweed.
At angular point, a sacred joint,
    The horned confluence meets.

Flood suits the colour of the spate
    To brown or glowing white,
Two step the dance a hundred yards
    Before they will unite.

As arrowheads that needle by
    When fingers part the grass,
Or blade and spear which taper
    A point in time to pass,

So the sharp pace mixes rivers
    Reeling with tanged horn,
And birls the pirn. His tractor overturns,
    Walter rolls up reborn.

NEWSTEAD 2000

Eight hundred cavalry
riding without stirrups
wheeled to obey the beacon on the hilltop.

'By the right!' The inmost stayed
knee to knee, chamfron to chamfron,
'Dress up! dress up! Canter on!'

They had buried all the good tools
and a ton of unused iron nails.
Southwards, they went away,

losing intaglio rings from their heyday,
abandoning the inscribed building stone,
'Twentieth Valerian and Victorious Legion.'

Then what delayed
beyond tonight
someone blotting out torchlight

and these impalpable shades?

BEMERSYDE'S WELCOME

Storm races up. On a day
Like this, the big tree went down in the young corn
And the cockpheasant blew clean off the birdtray.
Maybe it is man's doing, now the rolling
Air shapes swift movement above, clouds roiling.

Soon a century ends. In weather
Oscillating wildly, these troubled mixed times
Of a thousand and a thousand run together.
High wind whistles round the old stronghold. It keeps
Warm welcome, and Dante's words that never sleep.

The turbulence is held in check
Down the strait slope, going into the gorge
Where a great torque sits calmly on the cliff's neck.
Three-quarters circle, the bight, the riverbend has scope
To twirl and twist its loop of wiry rope,

Tightly wound, running and curling in,
A glowing mass beneath the hanging woods.
Ember of iridescence. The colour of resin
But wide and swift. A joy, a jewel,
Dusky Tweed of pot-like pools

That flow against the streams of time,
With windflow on backblow upstream,
Makes away from the sea, river of the mind.
As man in his few metres of atmosphere
Picks his steps in the windy gowl with fear

So, angling last century in the Haly Wele
For the deadly taking moment, the boatman waded
Up to his armpits, towing the keel,
Treading the secret shallows. He held the sway
To the very centre, where he knew his way.

THE RANT OF THE TROWS

From weirs and caulds to streamy pools,
The rocky foss past, come famous casts,
By Orchard Heads to Nethern Heads:
The Side Straik and Elshie Stream,
The Red Stane, the Laird's aim,
The Dark Shore, the noble Doors,
A rippling reach, tough fins in each,
With a brisk curl on the water's whirl.

By turmoil, rapid and the flat,
the out-bring will snap and sing
through deep Trows, the rare Trows.

A wizard's foot set the current's root,
The print of it in the gorge gullet,
An active lad might leap dryshod.
Who lacks belief comes to grief
In the slit defile, a devil's smile,
The four troughs deep enough,
The narrow Trows, the rapid Trows.

The rock rent, the torn vents
Fling a bar, form a scar
Of cleft kerb, the stone curb
Where time is nicked to the quick
By sharp Trows, the bare Trows.

The ardent rate concentrates
The whole force to gush hoarse
To say it, to vary wit
In water vow from bold pow.
The trap rock, the pelt shock
Rings the Trows, scotch-snap Trows,
Makerstoun's Trows below Mertoun.

PRESSEN HILL

Somewhere here, there's water still to find,
contained in earth's crust from earlier geologic time.
True connate water is very rare,
as if a pyramid had trapped the ancient air.
Who would breathe it, who would drink
the element held within its brink?
And breathing, drinking, broach for us then
the first word of the biosphere to men.

SCALE

A child of the wild
upland moors I grew up
by streams you might just step across:
like them, a little speaking daughter of the moss.

I reeled in the field
lop-sided with the salmon-rod,
practising casts in an acre of grass
and wondering where was a water this vast.

Nearing the sea,
'River Tweed's a grand river,'
he said, and I looked out thirstily:
more than enough, the fullness of her mystery.

THE CANTO OF TWEED'S MOUTH

Walking from source to sea
draws a lifeline's journey.
Spray spread
on my head,
foam on my body,
I leave it on me.
Well-drinker, bank-walker, my boat
is ottering down on the river's long rope.

Tueda, who has one of the old names,
so old there's no meaning to explain,
you know it's a suspicious time, we sue
those who boil the oceans down for glue
and we fear the glassful from the tap.
Swallow our despair, rise up,
open your mouth, the origin of things,
the first voice to speak or sing,
foretell fresh water for us,
bearer of youths and of harvests.
Brand your flood-shape into the rocks,
turn full-face to us, wavy locks.

'Far from me, Tweedsmuir,
the midmoss of man's cure,
far from me, Fruid and Quair,
the first waters of Scotland there.'

*   *   *

By braided channel, riverbed of the brain,
man and land she plaits again,
slows to a big lowland waterway
where pool and rapid die away.

Tides back the water up, centuries of war
cross the narrow haven's shallow bar,
sea-wealth under bastion and parapet,
the water-walls of beleaguered Berwick.

Give her the love-talk of the names,
colours brought down in spate's champagne.
From long Slake to old Scotsgate,
Hang-a-dyke Neuk and Longheughs,
slip and quays, Gillies Braes,
groynes and piers, Breakneck Stairs,
Calot Shad for diving shag,
Back Gut Stell and Conqueror's Well
to the last land, Out Water Batt,
Tueda's fish-mouth opens for that.
She lifts her head from the nets, flows
by and touches us as she goes.

From the uplands and high moors
to the broad valley and seashores,
space! And the river signs her course:
form is the diagram of force.
Water propels a wave, an impetus;
whatever is in nature, is also in us.

Play the note and say her name
before the world shall change again,
ruined it can never be
while Tweed runs to the sea.

NOTES ON THE POEMS

The forms of the poems have a relationship with the river, thus shaping the verses. Tweed's beauty is in the variety of its landscape and in the music of its water.

UPLAND SONG

Close to the source, moorland birds call and a tractor engine sounds.

'coulter', the iron blade in front of the ploughshare.
'dyker', a builder of drystone walls.
'shaw', a small natural wood.
'brig', the single-span bridge at Tweedsmuir.
'white ground', local definition of good pasture.

STREAM RHYTHM

The young Tweed is joined by many tributary streams, burns and rivulets. The place-names here are a mixture of Welsh, Gaelic and Scots, which, if translated, still describe the location with accuracy today.

THE BELTANE FORDING

A Beltane festival is held each year in Peebles. People celebrate their past and mark out their territory for the future by their horsemanship when crossing the river.

'White Stane', a glacial erratic boulder on the edge of the town.
'paved causeway', the fording-places are paved under the water.
'Carbantorigon', the chariot-slope, a town of the Selgovae, it flourished 2000 years ago, and was probably situated near Easter Happrew farm, close to the influx of Lyne Water.

OLD HOWFORD

An old ford between Cardrona and Traquair, by the forest.

MRS COCKBURN'S FAVOURITE

Around Traquair there are places which are considered to be good or bad, fortunate or unlucky, often because of events which have happened there in the past. The ruinous tower houses at the mouth of every defile, for example, have known violent scenes.

This sonnet praises a good place, the favourite of Mrs Cockburn, farmer's wife at Damhead. Her husband goes ahead on his four-stroke to open the gates, then she rides away over a wide green sward facing Plora, where James Hogg's Kilmeny disappeared to 'the land of vision'. The river is left far below and the undulating hills appear like nowhere else, line after line.

WALTER ELLIOT'S REEL

'Ettrick coming down is drumlie, Tweed is clear, and the two colours, the two currents, can be seen flowing side by side but not mixing for quite a way below the new bridge.'
Walter Elliot, timber contractor and historian.

At the confluence of Ettrick and Tweed, there is a prehistoric settlement right at the water's edge, where Walter finds flint arrowheads, scrapers and fishing net weights each year.

'birl', to whirl round rapidly; to revolve as in a dance; to pour wine for someone.
'pirn', a spool; the reel of a fishing rod.
'chert', a variety of quartz resembling jasper.

NEWSTEAD 2000

The site of the Roman fort and camps at Trimontium, garrisoned by *Legio XX Valeria Victrix* and auxiliary cavalry regiments, extends over 200 acres near Newstead village. Finds from the last first century AD include bronze and iron helmet-masks, and a 'chamfron' or pony-cap. This is a horse's leather headpiece with tooled surface designs of circles and leaves, and brass-headed studs (National Museum of Antiquities, Edinburgh). Recently, the Trimontium Trust has been formed to protect the site.

'beacon', the beacon-fire from the signal station on Eildon Hill North.

'Dress up!', a command to straighten up the course of a line of cavalry, with which I grew familiar when riding out with the Maharajah's Mounted Company, Mysore, South India.

'intaglio', semi-precious stones from a seal ring. Master engravers made the intaglio a jewel to be admired. Fine examples from Trimontium can be seen in the National Museum of Antiquities.

BEMERSYDE'S WELCOME

Bemersyde, the home of Earl Haig's family, perches above a turn in the river where there are cliffs and overhanging woods. The present Earl is one of Scotland's renowned painters, and his Countess is an artist in embroidery. The Countess is Venetian, and keeps her father's copy of Dante's *Divine Comedy* in the house.

'Welcome', a fiddle tune played to welcome a guest: here Bemersyde itself is welcoming and the river valley gives shelter on the stormiest of days.

'torque', a collar of twisted metal, in bronze or gold, worn by ancient Celts as a sign of rank.

'dusky Tweed', below Leader Water, the Tweed is coloured in flood-time by the wash from red sandstone, and remains clouded for some distance.

'Haly Wele', a famous salmon-pool where huge fish rest comfortably.

THE RANT OF THE TROWS

One of the great beats of the river is the stretch from Mertoun to Makerstoun, with pools and casts well-known to salmon-fishermen. Running water was fatal to a wizard's powers: Merlin's drowning in the Tweed at Drumelzier is one example. Here, near Makerstoun, Michael Scot the wizard (or intellectual) attempted to bridle the Tweed by casting a curb of stone across it. As he was completing the work, he stepped out, but left one foot in the water. Immediately the currents rushed in on the place, forming the Trows, or troughs.

'rant', boisterous talk; a lively tune or song; a title for a dance tune.

The poem is a rant with internal rhymes that mimic the shape and sound of v-shaped troughs.

PRESSEN HILL

Pressen Hill is near Wark, with its motte and bailey. From here downstream, the place-names on the river are Anglo-Saxon.

'connate water', subterranean water, locked in since the formation of the earth, it is not part of the everyday hydrologic cycle, neither in rain nor river, spring nor sea.

SCALE

By Norham and Paxton, approaching the sea, the tides affect the river and hold it back so that it rises upon itself. The river is in its amplitude.

THE CANTO OF TWEED'S MOUTH

Tweed appears on old maps as *Tueda*, and as *Tuuide*, in medieval texts. The meaning of the name Tweed is obscure. It was probably obscure to the Celts when they first settled here. What is certain is that the pre-Celtic population of Scotland, and the Celts after them, regarded rivers as divine, and those old sacred names of rivers are the most durable in Europe, outlasting cultures and eras.

The Gaelic hero Cuchulainn, coming to the ford of the river Cronn and seeing the host of his enemies approaching, prayed to the river to help him fight them. The river rose until it was in the tops of the trees. And for us now, the river is a source of life, a key to our survival beyond this century. The River Tweed is a sign of the re-creative power of nature and of time.

LIST OF ILLUSTRATIONS

Page 6. Smailholm Tower, built in the early 16th century, is now in the care of the State. With its seven foot thick walls and its commanding position it made the perfect refuge and beacon tower.

Page 15. Neidpath Castle, a tower house dating from the 14th century, is now owned by the Wemyss family. The surrounding woodlands were grown to replace the great trees sold as timber by the 4th Duke of Queensbury in 1795 for which he was pilloried by Wordsworth in a famous sonnet.

Page 17. The railway bridge at Berwick-on-Tweed was designed by Robert Stevenson and built between 1847–50 at a total cost of £253,000.

Page 20. A mature pine plantation near Cardrona, taken in winter on a hillside above the Tweed.

Page 23. St Mary's Loch, whose waters flow into the Yarrow, one of the Tweed's tributaries.

Page 25. Talla Waterfall near the source of the Tweed, above Talla Reservoir.

Page 27. Where the velocity of the stream is high, the water rushes over the boulders with elemental force. The rocks are smoothed and rounded by its movement.

Page 29. A dramatic shot on a hillside above the Tweed showing swift surface runoff and erosion of the slope on a ridge topped by forestry.

Page 31. This bridle path leading through the woods brings you to a gate that will open onto the wide expanse of the Border hills.

Page 33. 'The Meeting Pool' where the Ettrick meets the Tweed is a popular fishing place. Above the confluence stands The Rink, an iron age hill-fort.

Page 35. An unusual view of part of the triple-peaked Eildon Hills, an area long associated with tales both historical and magical.

Page 37. A bend in the Tweed near Bemersyde, seen below Sir Walter Scott's favourite viewing place where it is said his horses stopped of their own accord.

Page 39. A lovely stretch of the Tweed near Mertoun Bridge by St Boswells where the fishing is first class both in autumn and in spring. The buildings opposite once formed part of a mill.

Page 41. These river grasses grow near many parts of the Tweed but are particularly character-istic of the rich lands of the Merse.

Page 43. A fisherman's boat on the Tweed below Kelso near the famous Maxwheel pool.

Page 45. Ripple marks over the sand, caused by the ceaseless flow of both the Tweed and tides at the mouth of the river.